Encouraging Others

by Brienna Rossiter

FOCUS READERS

PIONEER

www.focusreaders.com

Focus Readers is distributed by North Star Editions:
sales@northstareditions.com | 888-417-0195

Produced for Focus Readers by Red Line Editorial.

Photographs ©: Shutterstock Images, cover, 1, 10, 12, 15, 17, 18, 20; iStockphoto, 4, 6, 8

Library of Congress Cataloging-in-Publication Data
Names: Rossiter, Brienna, author.
Title: Encouraging others / by Brienna Rossiter.
Description: Lake Elmo, MN: Focus Readers, 2021. | Series: Spreading
  kindness | Includes index. | Audience: Grades 2-3
Identifiers: LCCN 2020033631 (print) | LCCN 2020033632 (ebook) | ISBN
  9781644936832 (hardcover) | ISBN 9781644937198 (paperback) | ISBN
  9781644937914 (pdf) | ISBN 9781644937556 (ebook)
Subjects: LCSH: Encouragement--Juvenile literature. | Helping
  behavior--Juvenile literature. | Kindness--Juvenile literature.
Classification: LCC BF637.E53 R67 2021 (print) | LCC BF637.E53 (ebook) |
  DDC 155.4/192--dc23
LC record available at https://lccn.loc.gov/2020033631
LC ebook record available at https://lccn.loc.gov/2020033632

Printed in the United States of America
Mankato, MN
012021

About the Author

Brienna Rossiter is a writer and editor who lives in Minnesota. She loves cooking food and being outside.

Table of Contents

Chapter 1

Showing Support

Encouraging someone means giving that person help and **support**. As a result, that person feels less **lonely** or less sad. You help them feel hopeful or brave instead.

There are many ways to encourage others. You can visit a neighbor. You can cheer for a friend's team. You can speak kindly. Or you can give a hug. These actions show that you care.

Chapter 2

Staying Positive

Everyone has bad days. People may want to **complain** or give up. But you can help them stay **positive**. Remind people of what they have and what they can do.

Sometimes people make mistakes. Don't laugh or make fun of them. Instead, focus on what they did well. Tell them they were brave to try. And encourage them to try again.

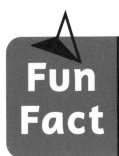

Fun Fact

Making mistakes is how people learn and grow.

Chapter 3

Using Words

You can use your words to encourage others. Tell people when they do a good job. And thank them if they help you. It shows you **appreciate** what they did.

Don't say things that are rude or mean. Instead, use kind words. Try to make others feel happy. Say why you like them.

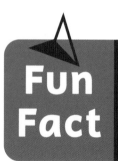

Fun Fact

Words have great power to help or hurt.

Encouraging Words

Well done!

You can do it!

That was brave!

Great idea!

Good teamwork!

I'm proud of you!

Write a Note

Writing is a great way to encourage others. First, choose a friend or family member. Think of what you like about this person. What does he or she do well? Next, write a note. Explain what you like or **admire**. Then, give your note to the person.

Chapter 4

Using Actions

Your actions can encourage others. If people are having a hard time, offer to help. You can help them solve a problem. Or you can do a **chore** for them.

Sometimes just being with people is enough to make them feel better. You help them remember they are not alone. And you show that you care about how they feel.

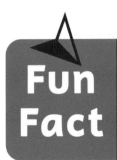

Fun Fact

People often send cards to show they are thinking about someone.

FOCUS ON
Encouraging Others

Write your answers on a separate piece of paper.

1. Write a sentence describing one way you can encourage a friend.

2. Do you feel more encouraged by people's words or actions? Why?

3. What should you do if people make mistakes?
   - A. Laugh at them.
   - B. Pretend you don't see them.
   - C. Encourage them to try again.

4. Why would spending time with people encourage them?
   - A. It can help them be less brave.
   - B. It can help them be more lonely.
   - C. It can help them be less lonely.

Answer key on page 24.

Glossary

admire
To like someone a lot and think he or she is a good person.

appreciate
To be thankful for something.

chore
A job that people do regularly around the home.

complain
To say something is unfair or say you don't like it.

lonely
Feeling sad as a result of being alone.

positive
Focused on the good parts of something.

support
Help or comfort given to another person.

To Learn More

BOOKS

Lopez, Elizabeth Anderson. *Fantastic Kids: Helping Others*. Huntington Beach, CA: Teacher Created Materials, 2018.

Murphy, Frank. *Stand Up for Caring*. Ann Arbor, MI: Cherry Lake Publishing, 2019.

NOTE TO EDUCATORS

Visit **www.focusreaders.com** to find lesson plans, activities, links, and other resources related to this title.

Index